DiscoverRoo
An Imprint of Pop!
popbooksonline.com

**Hauntings**

# HAUNTED PLACES

by Elizabeth Andrews

**abdobooks.com**

Published by Pop!, a division of ABDO, PO Box 398166, Minneapolis, Minnesota 55439. Copyright © 2022 by Abdo Consulting Group, Inc. International copyrights reserved in all countries. No part of this book may be reproduced in any form without written permission from the publisher. DiscoverRoo™ is a trademark and logo of Pop!.

Printed in the United States of America, North Mankato, Minnesota.

102021
012022

 **THIS BOOK CONTAINS RECYCLED MATERIALS**

Cover Photos: Shutterstock Images, (photo and pattern)

Interior Photos: Shutterstock Images, 1, 5, 6, 10, 14, 23, 25; UBC Library/Wikimedia, 9; Save the Children Canada/Wikimedia, 13; Royasfoto73/Wikimedia, 17; Aarau City Museum, album Gysi 1897/Wikimedia, 18; Harry Shepherd/Stringer/Getty Images, 19; Universal History Archive/UIG/Shutterstock, 20; p.portal.photo/ Alamy Stock Photo, 26; Moviestore/Shutterstock, 29

Editor: Tyler Gieseke
Series Designer: Laura Graphenteen

Library of Congress Control Number: 2021943408

**Publisher's Cataloging-in-Publication Data**

Names: Andrews, Elizabeth, author.

Title: Haunted places / by Elizabeth Andrews

Description: Minneapolis, Minnesota : Pop!, 2022 | Series: Hauntings | Includes online resources and index

Identifiers: ISBN 9781098241254 (lib. bdg.) | ISBN 9781644946787 (pbk.) | ISBN 9781098241957 (ebook)

Subjects: LCSH: Haunted places--Juvenile literature. | Ghosts--Juvenile literature. | Ghost towns--Juvenile literature. | Ghost Stories--Juvenile literature.

Classification: DDC 133.12--dc23

# WELCOME TO DiscoverRoo!

Pop open this book and you'll find QR codes loaded with information, so you can learn even more!

Scan this code* and others like it while you read, or visit the website below to make this book pop!

## popbooksonline.com/haunted-places

*Scanning QR codes requires a web-enabled smart device with a QR code reader app and a camera.

# TABLE OF CONTENTS

# CHAPTER 1

# WATCH YOUR STEP

Walking through a cemetery at night would frighten anyone. Who knows what is peering from behind headstones? What is causing the hairs on the back of your neck to stand up? Maybe the spirits of the

**WATCH A VIDEO HERE!**

*Cemeteries are known for making people feel uneasy, especially on dark, foggy nights.*

dead are gathering near you without your notice. Some places just have a spooky feeling to them.

*If you see a perfectly shaped mound,*
*it may be a burial ground.*

Over time certain places can collect

spirits and **supernatural** energies. This

can be caused by powerful events.

Battlefields from wars long past are

haunted by the fear and bloodshed.

Houses where violent deaths occurred

might still be home to the ghosts of the victims.

A few hills in the woods may not seem too frightening. But they could be ancient burial mounds. The spirits of the people buried a thousand years ago are resting quietly. There's no telling what could happen if they are disturbed.

Haunted places are exciting. They have stories to tell. It's important to watch where you step. If you stumble upon a spot with odd energy, treat it with respect. It might be home to restless ghosts.

## CHAPTER 2

# WASHED AWAY

On March 11, 2011, Japan experienced a large natural disaster. The Great East Japan earthquake shifted the earth off the coast of Japan. It caused a **tsunami**. Waves as tall as 132 feet (40 m) hit the

**LEARN MORE HERE!**

*Tsunamis pick up everything in their paths when they wash ashore.*

northeastern part of the island. The

destruction was devastating. Land was

flooded six miles (10 km) in from the

shore. The waves washed away homes,

businesses, and farmland.

# 2011 EARTHQUAKE AND TSUNAMI

Tōhoku was the area most affected by the earthquake and tsunami. This northern area of Japan has not updated its way of life as quickly as places like Tokyo. The people here are surrounded by mountains and forests. They live rural, traditional lives centered around farming and family.

Tōhoku

Sea of Japan

JAPAN

Tokyo

PACIFIC OCEAN

KEY

 earthquake

 tsunami

 capital

Nearly 16,000 people died because of the tsunami. Many survivors lost their entire families. Sometimes the waves carried bodies of loved ones miles from where they last were. Families had to search for days or weeks to find them. All the death led to supernatural happenings in the Tōhoku region.

The people of Tōhoku are very attached to their ancestors. It is important that they pay proper respects to anyone they love who died. It is tradition to hold ceremonies and cremate the dead.

Sadly, the tsunami's destruction made that impossible. It took a long time to find bodies. The region was also running on little power. The equipment needed to cremate the bodies couldn't be used. So, survivors had to break tradition and bury their dead.

That might be what led to so many ghost sightings. The people of Tōhoku were unable to find comfort when saying goodbye to their loved ones in such an

improper way. The souls of the dead

couldn't find peace this way either. So,

they wandered looking for their bodies.

Some didn't even realize they were

dead. The survivors felt guilty. Maybe

this opened them up to the possibility

of ghosts.

*It took over a year to remove the tsunami debris.*

*Some survivors claim to see the eyes of ghosts in pools of liquid like tea or rain.*

Taxi drivers in the area said that

months after the tsunami, they would

pick up people and drive them to

homes that had been washed away.

When the drivers turned around to ask

about it, their passengers would be

gone. Another spirit visits her old friend's

home. She's invited in to sit and have tea, only to disappear before it can be poured. A damp spot on her chair is all that remains.

People began reporting possessions after the tsunami too. One man suddenly started growling and rolling on the ground after seeing the destruction from the waves. He was violent and spoke about the dead. One girl said she could feel spirits entering her. Perhaps it's the survivors' grief making them see things. Or maybe, the spirits are really there.

# DEAD BUT NEVER GONE

Hiding in the city of Louisville, Kentucky, is the Waverly Hills Sanatorium. A sanatorium is a place where people with a long-term illness can go to get medical attention and hopefully heal.

LEARN MORE HERE!

Waverly Hills was built in 1910 to care for people with tuberculosis. It is a disease that hurts the lungs. Since there was no cure, few people recovered from tuberculosis. In the 1900s, it was the leading cause of death in the United States.

The US was going through a tuberculosis **epidemic** when Waverly opened. The disease spread easily. So, the government built places for sick patients. Those places needed to be far

*Families were sometimes forced apart when a member came down with tuberculosis.*

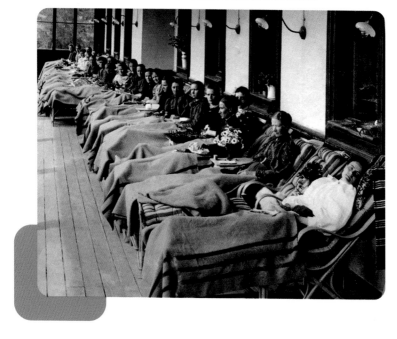

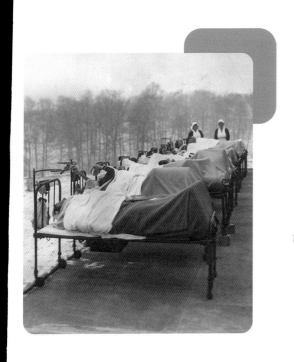

*Fresh air and rest were the best ways to treat people with tuberculosis.*

away from people and have lots of fresh air. Waverly Hills had its own post office. Doctors and nurses lived on the property. Workers even grew their own food. Once people got to Waverly Hills, they would rarely get to rejoin the regular world.

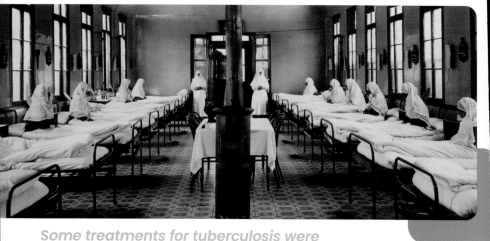

*Some treatments for tuberculosis were very painful, but sometimes helped.*

As many as 10,000 people may have died at the sanatorium during the 50 years it was open. Visitors of Waverly Hills today go to the **abandoned** property looking for ghosts.

The most famous ghost is that of a little boy who died, named Timmy. Wandering the third floor, he tries to get people to play with him. He's known to

make a blue ball appear and bounce.

Some ghost hunters bring their own ball

for Timmy to play with.

Ghostly figures have been captured

on camera at Waverly Hills. Many people

believe the most photographed ghost

is that of a homeless man who lived in

Waverly after it was abandoned. He and

his white dog died after falling down an

elevator shaft.

Doctors and nurses used an underground hallway to move dead bodies at Waverly. That way the patients wouldn't see all the people who were dying of their same illness. Ghost hunters call the hallway "the body chute." There, people see shadow figures running toward them in the dark. They also feel sudden bursts of cold and warm air. All around Waverly, doors slam on their own and screams of pain can be heard. There is little rest in these walls.

*The body chute can be toured when visiting Waverly Hills.*

# CHAPTER 4

# FIT FOR A KING

High in the mountains of Estes Park,

Colorado, is the Stanley Hotel. It was

built in 1909 by a man named Freelan

Oscar Stanley. He and his wife Flora

**COMPLETE AN ACTIVITY HERE!**

*Freelan was sick with tuberculosis when he first visited Estes Park. He credited his recovery to the fresh air.*

loved the town of Estes Park. They built

the hotel so more people could come

enjoy the mountain air. The Stanley

Hotel is still operating today. It is

known for its beautiful location and its

**supernatural** guests.

*Sometimes guests see ghosts in the mirrors that line the grand staircase.*

Freelan died in 1940, but he still hangs around the hotel. Guests say his ghost spends time in the game room and bar. He is sometimes seen leaning on the front desk checking reservations.

Flora Stanley never left either. She likes to play her old piano that sits in the front entry. There is a large mirror hanging above it. Some people say they have seen Flora in it.

**DID YOU KNOW?** The Stanley has a pet cemetery. Ghosts of a golden retriever and a fluffy white cat are seen around the hotel.

In 1920 the hotel had a gas leak. A maid named Elizabeth was lighting a candle in room 217. The mixture of fire and gas caused an explosion. Elizabeth survived and kept working at the Stanley until she died. But people say her ghost settled in room 217. She doesn't like male guests, so

## THE SHINING

Stephen King is one of the most famous authors of scary stories. He and his wife stayed in room 217 at the Stanley in 1974. King says that his stay inspired his most famous book, *The Shining*. It's about a family staying in the Overlook Hotel. They are **tormented** by strange spirits and the father goes crazy. King's novel helped make the Stanley Hotel famous.

*Jack Nicholson and Shelley Duvall starred in* The Shining *film.*

### THE
# SHiNiNG

she packs their bags and puts them by the door. She pushes unmarried couples apart who share a bed in the room.

Visitors to the Stanley Hotel know what they're getting into when they make reservations. Most are thrilled to spend time in the mountains. They are also just as excited to share space with the ghosts!

# MAKING CONNECTIONS

### TEXT-TO-SELF

Would you ever go looking for haunted places? If so, what would you hope to find?

### TEXT-TO-TEXT

Have you read any other books about hauntings or ghosts? What did they have in common with these stories?

### TEXT-TO-WORLD

Japanese have funeral traditions. Can you think of any other cultures that follow traditions or ceremonies when saying goodbye to their dead?

# GLOSSARY

**abandon** — left without protection or care.

**ancestor** — a family member from an earlier time.

**cremate** — to expose a dead body to flame and heat. The body breaks down to pieces as small as ash.

**devastate** — to bring ruin, disorder, and helplessness.

**epidemic** — the rapid spread of a disease among many people.

**supernatural** — something that exists beyond what is observable.

**torment** — extreme suffering of the mind or body.

**tsunami** — a group of powerful ocean waves that can destroy areas.

# INDEX

# ONLINE RESOURCES
## popbooksonline.com

Scan this code* and others like it while you read, or visit the website below to make this book pop!

## popbooksonline.com/haunted-places

*Scanning QR codes requires a web-enabled smart device with a QR code reader app and a camera.